POWER-GLIDE

FOREIGN
LANGUAGE COURSES

Power-Glide
French Junior
Adventure Guide

Levels II

by

Robert W. Blair

This product would not have been possible without the assistance of many people. The help of those mentioned below was invaluable.

Editorial, Design and Production Staff

Instructional Design: Robert Blair, Ph.D.

Project Coordinator: James Blair

Development Manager: David Higginbotham

Story Writer: Natalie Prado

Cover Design: Guy Francis

Contributing Editors: Gretchen Hilton, Emily Spackman, Ann Dee Knight, Heather Monson, Amelia Taylor

Audios Voices: Ali Seable Durham, Erin Sorensen, Peter Enyeart, Art Burnah, Christel Marie Secrist, David Higginbotham

Illustrator: Apryl Robertson

Translators: Christel Marie Secrist

Musicians: Geoff Groberg, Rob Bird

Audio Recording, Editing and Mixing: Rob Bird

Power-Glide Foreign Language Courses
1682 W 820 N, Provo, UT 84601
(9/01)

Contents

A Note to Parents

Basic Course Objectives

The major goal of this course is to keep children excited about communicating in another language. The adventure story, the variety of activities, and the simplified teaching methods employed in the course are all designed to make learning interesting and fun.

This course is primarily for children 2nd through 4th grade. Course activities are designed specifically with these learners in mind and include matching games, story telling, speaking, drawing, creative and deductive thinking, acting, and guessing—all things which children do for fun!

Ultimately, children who complete the course can expect to understand an impressive amount of French, including common French phrases, complete French sentences, French numbers, rhymes, and questions. They will also be able to understand stories told all or mostly in French, to retell these stories themselves using French, and to make up stories of their own using words and sentence patterns they have learned.

Children who complete the course will be well prepared to continue learning with our other French courses, and they will have the foundation that will make learning at that level just as fun and interesting, albeit more challenging, than in this course.

Teaching Techniques

This course allows your children to learn by doing, to learn through enjoyable experiences. The idea is to put the experience first and the explanation after. This is important to note because it is directly opposite to how teaching—and especially foreign language teaching—is traditionally done. Typically foreign language teachers spend the majority of their time explaining complex grammar and syntax rules, and drilling students on vocabulary. In this traditional mode, rules and lists come first and experience comes last. Learning experientially, on the other hand, simulates the natural language acquisition process of children.

When children learn their native languages apparently effortlessly in early childhood, it is not through the study of grammar rules and vocabulary lists. Rather, they learn the words for things around them simply by listening to others, and they intuitively grasp an amazing amount of grammar and syntax in the same way. By using activities that simulate natural language acquisition, it is not only possible, but normal for children to learn a new language quickly and enjoy doing it!

Specifically, this course motivates your children to learn French by providing learning experiences in the form of matching games, story telling exercises, drawing exercises, singing and acting, and other fun activities aimed at developing functional language comprehension and speaking ability. These activities contrast markedly with the exercises in more traditional courses, which tend to focus exclusively on learning some vocabulary, or on understanding very simple French sentences, without extending learning to the point of actually understanding and speaking the language. The language your children will acquire through this course will be more useful to them than language learned through traditional approaches, because knowledge gained in fun, rather than stressful, ways is much easier for children to retain and much more natural for them to use themselves.

Using the Course

This course is carefully designed so that it can be used either by children working primarily on their own or by parents and children working closely together. Complete instructions, simple enough to be easily followed by children, are included on the audios. Parents or other adults can enhance the course significantly by acting as facilitators: reviewing instructions, encouraging creativity and course participation, providing frequent opportunities for children to display what they have learned, rewarding effort and accomplishment, and providing enthusiasm. Keep in mind that much of the real learning takes place as you interact with your children during and after the course learning experiences.

Perhaps the most important of the above ways parents can help their children is to give them an audience for their new skills. In order to facilitate this invaluable help, we have added a new feature to the Children's Level II French Course. At the end of each activity or story we have included suggestions for a Performance Challenge. One goal of Power-Glide courses is to teach students to produce the target language creatively and independently. The new Performance Challenge feature will help children do just that. These additional exercises will increase your child's fluency, pronunciation, and confidence in the target language, as well as give you the opportunity to be directly involved in the learning process. Encourage your children to use as much French as possible and give them the audience they need to perform for. Remind your students not to worry about mistakes. Rather, encourage them to review any words they may struggle with and make sure they feel comfortable with the current material before moving to the next lesson.

Using the resources provided in the course book and on the audios, an adult learning facilitator does not need to know French or how to teach it in order to be a great learning partner. In fact, one of the most enjoyable and effective ways to learn is together, as a team.

Parents or other adults who know French can, of course, supplement the materials in this course very effectively. A proficient bilingual teacher could, for example: (1) help children learn additional vocabulary by putting several objects on table and asking and answering questions about them, such as "What is this?" or "Where is the _____?", and so on; (2) create on-the-spot diglot-weave stories by reading illustrated children's books such as Silverstein's *Are You My Mother?*, putting key words (picturable nouns) into French, and asking questions about the story or its pictures partly or completely in French; (3) involve children in making and doing things (such as making a paper airplane or finding a hidden object) giving instructions all or partly in French.

We have added another new feature to this course that will make it easier to use. For each audio track, you will see a CD icon that includes the CD number and the track number. This will help you to easily find your place from lesson to lesson.

Benefits of Second Language Acquisition

Learning a second language has many benefits. Besides the obvious value of being able to understand and communicate with others, research in the United States and Canada in the 1970s and '80s has shown that learning a second language gives children a distinct advantage in general school subject areas. Seeing linguistic and cultural contrasts as they acquire a second language, children gain insight not only into the new language and cultures, but into their own language and culture as well.

Furthermore, a considerable amount of research has shown that learning a second language in childhood helps children learn to read and write their native language. Quite possibly the best phonics training a child can receive is to learn a language like French, because French spelling is quite phonetic: when one knows French, the spelling of a French word tells him or her how to pronounce it, and (with few exceptions) the sound of a French word tells him or her how to spell it. This carries over to English and helps children intuitively understand how language works.

Our Goal

Our goal at Power-Glide is to change the way the U.S. studies language. We want to produce foreign language speakers, not just studiers. This Children's Level II French Course effectively continues the road to speaking French. We hope you and your children will find delight in the ongoing adventure of learning another language.

The Adventure Begins

(Marseille)

◁))) Turn the audio on.

Narrator: Monday, 11 a.m. You peer out the window of the car as your family pulls up to the little cottage where your Grandpa Glen is staying. You can't believe that you are finally here, in Marseille, on the Mediterranean coast of France. Your Grandpa, who is here studying French art and folklore, invited your family to help him with his research. You are so excited! This is a wonderful opportunity to see a new country and practice your French. However, when you climb out and knock at the door, no one answers. Your parents seem concerned. A man who has been watching you from the yard next door approaches your parents and begins to speak to them in French. There is something about the neighbor that you don't like. You are not sure what it is.

Tony: Lisa, can you tell what they're saying?

Lisa: I'm not sure, Tony.

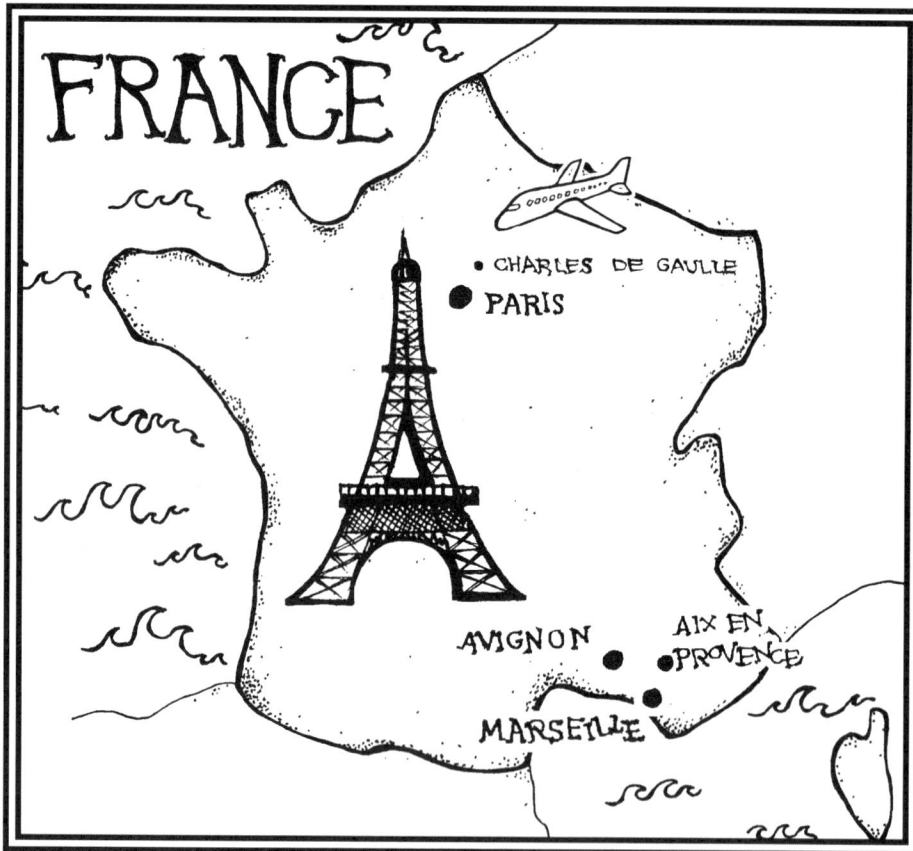

Malien: Grand-père Glen? Il n'est pas là. Ca fait trois jours qu'il est parti.

Tony: They must be talking about our Grandpa, I heard him say "Glen."

Lisa: I hope everything is all right.

Narrator: Your parents come back and explain that this man, Malien, is your Grandpa's next door neighbor. Grandpa Glen apparently had to leave town unexpectedly, and Malien has been picking up his mail for him. He also said that your distant cousin, Madeleine, had been visiting Grandpa Glen from Paris to help him with some French translations.

Lisa: That's strange. I wonder where Grandpa Glen has gone.

Tony: There's something funny going on here. I know it.

Lisa: Well, what do you think we should do?

Narrator: Your parents seem worried as well. The neighbor goes back to his yard, where he is gardening. Just then, the postman comes up and hands some letters to your parents. Your parents look through the letters and find one from Grandpa Glen! They open it and read it aloud.

Grandpa Glen: My dear Family: I am sorry I was not there to meet you. I hope you did not worry. I have been having an incredible adventure. It began a couple of weeks ago when, during the course of my research, I came across the diary of a certain Claude Revien, a famous art burglar from the early nineteenth century. In the diary, he confesses that he hid many of the priceless paintings he stole somewhere in the country, and that he left a trail of clues to find them, starting right here in Marseille! It was not until I was well into my search that I became aware that someone had discovered my plans to find the paintings and was trying to stop me. I need your help if I am to succeed! I cannot deny that this adventure could be dangerous. You will have to learn a great deal of French and use all of your courage and intelligence to track down the clues. It is too risky for me to tell you where I am, but luckily I hid a clue at the house that you can use to find me. I hid it very well. In order to find it, you must use the song I taught you once, "Sur le Pont D'Avignon." You must find me before noon on Thursday, or I will be forced to continue my search without you. I can wait no longer than Thursday. One last note—there is one person I know I can trust. She is the granddaughter of my cousin, who lives in Paris. Her name is Madeleine. She will be able to help you. I cannot tell you how important it is for you to begin your search immediately. Without your help, my quest will fail, and the paintings will fall into the hands of those seeking to ruin me. Be brave. Your Grandpa, Glen.

Narrator: Needless to say, you and your parents are very concerned about your grandpa. Your father says that if your grandpa is in trouble, it wouldn't do any good to go wandering around the country looking for him. Instead, he decides to alert the authorities and go speak to the other people in the neighborhood.

Lisa: But, Dad! What can we do to help?

Tony: Yeah, we want to find Grandpa Glen too. Is it okay if we try to find the clues?

Narrator: Your parents seem a bit skeptical, but you promise you will be careful. They say you may search around as long as you keep within sight of Grandpa's house. You promise. When your parents go inside to make some phone calls, you go over the letter again, and another piece of paper falls out.

Tony: What's this? It looks like some sort of puzzle.

🔈 **Turn the audio off.**

PERFORMANCE CHALLENGE:

Do you know where Marseille is? Find a map of the world, an encyclopedia, or a globe and locate Marseille.

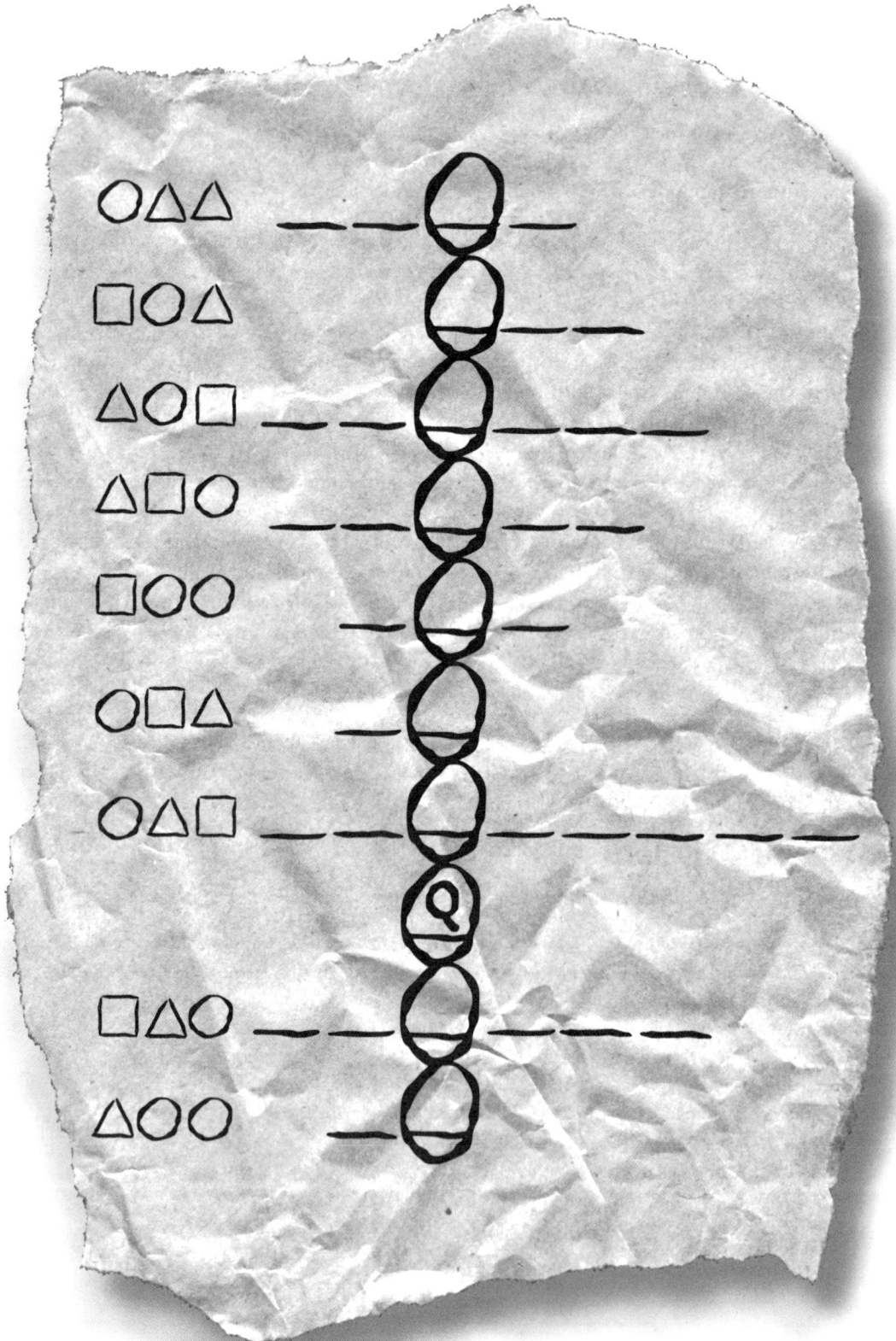

Grandpa Glen's Puzzle

Frére Jaques

(Ditties)

🔊))) **Turn the audio on.**

Track 2

Lisa: Well, I think the first thing we should do is speak to Madeleine. We should ask that neighbor, Malien, where she is.

Tony: Yeah, you're right. I'm a little bit nervous to speak in French, though. I'm not sure how much I remember.

Lisa: Yeah. It might be hard. How do we ask questions?

Tony: Hey... Do you remember that song that Grandpa taught us, "Frère Jaques?" It taught us a simple way to ask questions and give directions.

Lisa: That's right! How did it go?

Tony: Like this.

> Frère Jaques, frère Jaques,
>
> Dormez-vous? Dormez-vous?
>
> Sonnez les matines, sonnez les matines,
>
> Din, Din, Don!
>
> Din, Din, Don!

Lisa: That's right. I remember now.

> Frère Jaques, frère Jaques,
>
> Dormez-vous? Dormez-vous?
>
> Sonnez les matines, sonnez les matines,
>
> Din, Din, Don!
>
> Din, Din, Don!

Tony: Good. Let's sing it one time together.

Tony & Lisa:

Frère Jaques, frère Jaques,

Dormez-vous? Dormez-vous?

Sonnez les matines, sonnez les matines,

Din, Din, Don!

Din, Din, Don!

Lisa: Great!

🔊 **Turn the audio off.**

PERFORMANCE CHALLENGE:

Now that you have learned a new song, share your French with a parent, friend, or one of your brothers or sisters by teaching them the song. Remember to teach it in French and then translate the words into English if your partner does not understand French.

Sur le pont d'Avignon

(Ditties)

🔊))) **Turn the audio on.**

Track 3

Narrator: Monday, 1 p.m.

Lisa: So, should we go talk to Malien?

Tony: Well, I think that first we should look for the clue that Grandpa hid. It might be hard to find.

Lisa: Yeah, you're right. It could be anywhere in the house. Remember, he told us we would need to know the song "Sur le pont D'Avignon."

Narrator: You both begin to search the house.

Tony: Hey! Come and look at this.

Lisa: What? What is it?

Narrator: Tony points to the ceiling in the hallway, where there is a strange looking square, with the word "Messieurs" on it.

Tony: Isn't that strange? It must be some sort of door to an attic.

Lisa: Yeah. That word, "Messieurs," I think that's in the song.

Tony: How does the rest of the song go?

Lisa: Don't you remember? It went like this:

  Sur le pont d'Avignon,

  On y danse, on y danse,

  Sur le pont d'Avignon,

  On y danse tout en round.

  Les beaux messieurs font comme ça

  Et puis encore comme ça.

Tony: That's right! I remember now. Then, we go back to the chorus.

  Sur le pont d'Avignon,

  On y danse, on y danse,

  Sur le pont d'Avignon,

  On y danse tout en round.

  Les belles dames font comme ça

  Et puis encore comme ça.

Lisa & Tony:

> Sur le pont d'Avignon,
>
> On y danse, on y danse,
>
> Sur le pont d'Avignon,
>
> On y danse tout en round.
>
> Les cordonniers font comme ça
>
> Et puis encore comme ça.
>
> Sur le pont d'Avignon,
>
> On y danse, on y danse,
>
> Sur le pont d'Avignon,
>
> On y danse tout en round.

Tony: What should we do now?

Narrator: You both begin to search, and you find a ladder which you use to climb up to the ceiling. Pushing on the door marked "Messieurs," you crawl into a dark, dusty attic space. There are spiderwebs and shadows everywhere.

Lisa: It seems like the next word we would need to look for would be "dames." They're the next people who danced.

Tony: Look! There are words written on all of these old trunks.

Narrator: You look at the rows of trunks lined up and begin to wipe off the dust so that you can read the words written on them. Sure enough, the one nearest the door says "dames." You are almost to the back of the attic before you find the one marked "cordonniers." It is the oldest and most tattered of the trunks, and you hesitate to open it. Taking a deep breath, you push open the top, and laying on top is a beat-up, old spiral notebook.

Tony: Yes!

Lisa: We found it!

🔊 **Turn the audio off.**

PERFORMANCE CHALLENGE:

Now that you have learned a new song, share your French with a parent, friend, or one of your brothers or sisters by teaching them the song. Remember to teach it in French and then translate the words into English if your partner does not understand French.

The Three Pigs I

(Scatter Chart)

🔊 **Turn the audio on.**

5
Track 4

Narrator: Monday, 2 p.m.

Lisa: What does the notebook say?

Tony: It says, "Notes on the Revien Burglar." These must be the notes that Grandpa took when he was looking for clues! This will be very useful. Look what he wrote: "The first hint I received from the Revien memoirs took me to the Pont St-Bénézet at Avignon. I found that I would need to know a new story in French to find the next clue."

Lisa: It might take awhile to learn the story. What we need to do now is get to the Pont.

Narrator: You both scramble out of the attic and go searching for your parents. You are looking outside when you see Malien gardening again.

Tony: Quick, Lisa! Hide the letter and the notebook!

Malien: Vous, les enfants. Est-ce que le courrier est arrivé? Donnez-le moi.

Lisa: What is he saying?

Tony: I don't know.

Lisa: I don't trust him.

Tony: Neither do I. Let's go back inside the house.

Narrator: You go back inside, and sit at the table, looking over the notebook.

Tony: I guess that Mom and Dad must have gone into the neighborhood. What should we do until they get back?

Lisa: We need to learn that story.

Tony: You're right. It looks like Grandpa Glen wrote down some of the words we'll need to know. Let's take a look at them.

Look at the pictures on your workbook page and point to what you hear.

Track 5

s'échappe
escape

part
leaves

**la maison
de briques**
*the house of
bricks*

trés faim
very hungry

**le frére
numéro deux**
*brother
number two*

souffle
blows

**le frére
numéro trois**
*brother
number three*

tombe
falls down

arrive
comes

**la maison
de bois**
*the house of
sticks*

le pére
the father

**les petits
cochons**
little pigs

**la maison
de paille**
*the house of
straw*

**le frére
numéro un**
*brother
number one*

la mére
the mother

🔊 **Turn the audio off.**

PERFORMANCE CHALLENGE:

Choose five of the new words and pictures that you learned in the Scatter Chart. Show the pictures to a parent, friend, or one of your brothers or sisters and explain to them how you think the picture represents the words you have learned.

The Three Pigs I
(Match and Learn)

🔊 **Turn the audio on.**

Track 6

Lisa: Wow. I think I'm beginning to understand those words.

Tony: Me too. Okay. If we're going to get to the Pont, we'll probably need to find Madeleine. Let's ask Malien where she is.

Narrator: You both go outside to the edge of the yard and call to Malien.

Malien: Que voulez-vous maintenant?

Tony: Um... Monsieur. Uh... Madeleine?

Malien: Madeleine?

Tony: Oui, oui, Madeleine. Do you know where she is?

Malien: Je ne parle pas anglais. Elle est partie en promenade. Est-ce que vous me comprenez? Elle n'est pas ici.

Narrator: With that, Malien points down the road and goes inside his house.

Lisa: Oh, no. She must have just been here and then left. We're too late.

Tony: That's okay. It gives us a little more time. I'm sure she'll be back. Let's see if we can figure out some more words from that story.

Practice your new French vocabulary by pointing to the pictures when you hear the words.

Track 7

1.

2.

3.

4.

5.

6.

7.

8.

9.

10.

11.

12.

13.

14.

🔊 **Turn the audio off.**

PERFORMANCE CHALLENGE:

Draw a scene using the pictures you learned in your Match and Learn exercise. After you draw your picture, describe each part of the scene to a parent, friend, or one of your brothers or sisters. Remember to use as much French as you can to talk about your drawing.

The Three Pigs I

(Diglot Weave)

🔊)) **Turn the audio on.**

5 Track 8

Narrator: Just then your parents return, and you ask if you can run down the road to catch Madeleine before she leaves. Your parents have met Madeleine, and they agree. You hurry outside.

Tony: Do you think we can catch her?

Lisa: It's worth a try! Come on!

Narrator: You begin running down the road in the direction Malien pointed. A few minutes later you see in the distance a small, dark-haired young lady walking down the road.

Lisa: Do you think that's her?

Tony: There's only one way to find out.

Lisa: Bonjour! Bonjour, Mademoiselle!

Narrator: The young lady turns around. She has a pleasant face and warm eyes. She looks like she is about nineteen years old.

Madeleine: Bonjour, les enfants.

Lisa: Bonjour. Je m'appelle Lisa.

Tony: Et je m'appelle Tony.

Madeleine: Enchantée. Je m'appelle Madeleine.

Lisa: It's her! It's her! Do you speak English?

Madeleine: Oui, a little.

Narrator: You are very happy to meet your cousin. Madeleine walks back with you to Grandpa Glen's cottage. You tell her everything that has happened. With her help, you go through the story that Grandpa left you to learn.

I have copied down two versions of "The Three Little Pigs" for you. I felt you might be nervous about so many new words, so I'll give you a simpler version of the story first. Listen.

5 Track 9

Once upon a time there were 🐷🐷🐷 .

🐷🐷🐷 *were brothers,* 🐷①🐷②🐷③ .

This is their 🐷 ; *this is their* 🐷 .

This is ,

This is ,

This is ...the little brother...le petit frére.

Each of the build .

for ...le petit frére.

for , et

for .

comes.

He comes with much hunger.

He comes to .

... le petit frére., is in his .

blows.

falls: Crash!!

But fortunately escapes.

He runs to

Now comes to .

est in his .

is also in .

comes trés trés affamé.

.

The falls. Crash!!

But fortunately escape.

They run to .

Now comes

Le loup comes trés trés affamé..

The are in .

. again.

et .

But does not fall.

And so trés trés trés affamé.

Turn the audio off.

PERFORMANCE CHALLENGE:

There are four parts to this Performance Challenge:
1. Read the story silently to yourself.
2. Read the story aloud to yourself.
3. Read the story aloud to a parent, friend or one of your brothers and sisters.
4. Retell the story in your own words, using as much French as you can, to a parent, friend or one of your brothers or sisters. Don't worry if you can't remember every word. Do the best you can, and review the audio if you need to.

The Three Pigs I

(Review Questions)

🔊 Turn the audio on.

Track 10 **Narrator:** You are happy to find that Madeleine is as worried about your Grandpa as you are.

Madeleine: Vous voulez aider Glen? You need me to help you.

Tony: Oui, merci beaucoup. We need to go to the Pont St-Bénézet at Avignon.

Madeleine: Avignon? Venez avec moi.

Narrator: After your parents have given their permission, Madeleine takes you in her car to Avignon. It is not very far away, but while you are in the car, you review with each other what you remember from the story. Be sure to answer!

Note: Review questions are audio only.

🔊 Turn the audio off.

The Three Pigs II

(Scatter Chart)

Track 11

🔊 Turn the audio on.

Narrator: You arrive in Avignon. It is a smaller town than Marseille, but beautiful and charming. The Pont was once a large and impressive bridge, but, according to Madeleine, half of it fell into the river four hundred years ago! The ruins that are left are falling apart. Next to the bridge are piles of ancient bricks scattered around.

Tony: This bridge is so old! I don't know how we're ever going to find anything.

Lisa: Neither do I. And we're running out of time.

Tony: It must have something to do with the story. Let's take a break and see if we can learn any more. It would probably help us.

Lisa: You're right. Here are some new words.

Look at the pictures and words on your workbook page and point to what you hear.

Track 12

histoire
story

bonne idée
good idea

nuit
night

je pense
I think

appels
call out

jour
day

construire
to make

🔊 Turn the audio off.

PERFORMANCE CHALLENGE:

Choose five of the new words and pictures that you learned in the Scatter Chart. Show the pictures to a parent, friend, or one of your brothers or sisters and explain to them how you think the picture represents the words you have learned.

The Three Pigs II

(Match and Learn)

🔊))) **Turn the audio on.**

Track 13

Tony: Hey. What's that, next to the Pont?

Madeleine: That is called the Chapelle St-Nicolas. It is a very old church. I know the man who takes care of it, Michel.

Lisa: Should we knock on the door?

Narrator: Madeleine knocks. A friendly old man opens the door. He smiles. He and Madeleine speak to each other in French for a moment, then she introduces you.

Michel: Bonjour, les enfants.

Tony: Bonjour, Monsieur, je m'appelle Tony.

Lisa: Et je m'appelle Lisa.

Michel: Enchanté. Je m'appelle Michel. Est-ce que je peux vous aider ?

Tony: Oui, merci. Parlez-vous anglais?

Michel: Oui, a little.

Lisa: We are trying to help our Grandpa, Glen.

Michel: Ah, Glen. He was here about a week ago.

Tony: Do you know what he wanted?

Michel: Oui. He was looking for something on the bridge. I can show you where he was, if you like.

Lisa: Thank you.

Narrator: Michel takes you over to part of the ruined bridge. There is nothing there, except some scattered bricks, grass, and broken pieces of wood.

Tony: How will we know where to find the next clue?

Lisa: It must have something to do with the story. Let's see what we can figure out.

Practice these new words by pointing to the pictures when you hear the words. Look at picture box #1 in your workbook and point to what you hear.

Track 14

1.

2.

3.

4.

5.

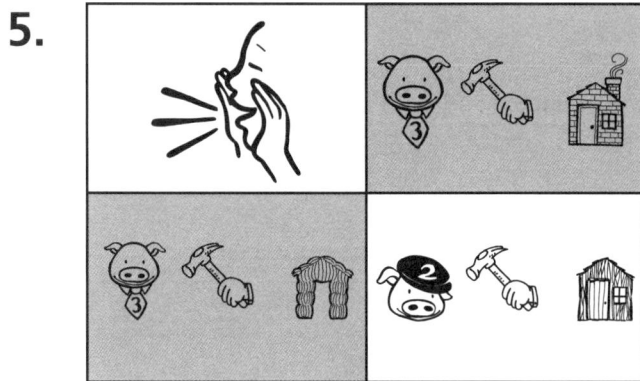

6.

7.

8.

🔇 **Turn the audio off.**

PERFORMANCE CHALLENGE:

Draw a scene using the pictures you learned in your Match and Learn exercise. After you draw your picture, describe each part of the scene to a parent, friend, or one of your brothers or sisters. Remember to use as much French as you can to talk about your drawing.

The Three Pigs II

(Diglot Weave)

🔊))) **Turn the audio on.**

Track 15

Lisa: We better hurry! Mom and Dad wanted us home in less than an hour. What does the notebook say?

Tony: Let me check. It says, "The memoirs indicated that the clue would be hidden in La maison ne tombait pas." That sounds familiar. It must be something in the story.

Lisa: You're right. Let's go over the story one more time, paying attention to anything that would have to do with the clue.

Track 16

Here is the second version I found of "The Three Little Pigs...Les trois petits cochons." Like other histoires of its kind, it begins with the words Once upon a time. In French we say it this way: Il était une fois. Once upon a time . . . Il était une fois

Now I'll begin l'histoire. Il était une fois trois cochons. This is leur père. C'est leur mère.

Les trois petits cochons are frères.

C'est le premier petit cochon, "le frère le plus âgé (le grand frère)."

C'est le deuxième petit cochon, "le frère suivant."

C'est le troisième petit cochon, "le frère le plus petit (le petit frère)."

Un jour, le plus petit des petits cochons dit, "I think I'll make a house....Je pense que je vais faire une maison.

I think I'll make a house of straw...Je pense que je vais faire une maison de paille."

Le grand frère says to him, "Oh, little brother that n'est pas a good idea....Oh, petit frère, ce n'est pas une bonne idée. Believe me, une maison de paille is no good...ce n'est pas bon."

Le plus petit cochon doesn't listen to his grand frère.

In a very short time... quand même he builds himself une maison de paille.

Against the advice of le grand frère, le plus petit cochon construit une maison de paille.

He is not very wise is he?

Le deuxième frère dit, "I think I'll make me a house too...Je pense aussi construire une maison. Je vais construire une maison de bois."

Le grand frère dit, "Ça ne marchera pas. Ça ne marchera pas. Believe me, Une maison de bois, ce n'est pas bon."

Le deuxième frère doesn't listen to his grand frère. Le deuxième frère quand même

builds himself une maison de bois. Against the advice of le grand frère, le deuxième

cochon construit une maison de bois. He is not very wise, is he?

Le frère le plus âgé est très intelligent.

Le grand frère dit, "Je pense aussi construire une maison, mais je pense construire une maison de briques."

Le frère le plus âgé est très intelligent. With great care, he construit une maison de briques, ni de paille ni de bois, mais de briques. Une maison solide!

Then, un jour, un loup arrive. He hasn't eaten for deux jours et il est très très hungry.

Il comes... arrive devant la maison de paille. Il renifle.

"Mmm, dans cette maison de paille, there is a delicious cochon."

Le loup goes près de la porte.

Il frappe à la porte (knock-knock), et calls out, "Petit cochon, petit cochon, let me entrer."

Le petit cochon dit, "No way...pas question, pas question! You... vous, are the big bad loup. Je ne vous laisserai pas entrer."

"Well then... Et bien," dit le loup, "If you don't let me in je vais souffler et souffler pour démolir ta maison."

Puis, le loup souffle fort, très fort, et démolit la maison.

Heureusement, le cochon s'échappe et court à la maison du frère numéro deux, à la maison de bois.

Le loup chases le petit cochon, but he can't catch him.

Le loup comes...arrive devant de la maison de bois.

He knows that there is at least one delicious cochon inside.

He goes up to the porte de la maison.

He frappe à la porte (knock-knock) et calls out, "Petit cochon, petit cochon, let me entrer."

"No way, no way !... Pas question, pas question! Vous êtes le méchant loup. Je ne vous laisserai pas entrer."

"Well then... Et bien, if you don't let me in je vais souffler et souffler...Je vais démolir ta maison."

Then le loup souffle très fort, et démolit la maison de bois du deuxième cochon.

Heureusement, les deux frères s'échappent et courent à la maison du grand frère, la maison de briques.

Le loup chases after les deux frères but he can't catch them.

Now le loup arrives devant la maison de briques.

He knows there are at least two delicious cochons dans la maison.

He frappe à la porte et dit, "Petit cochon, petit cochon, s'il vous plaît, laissez-moi entrer."

"Pas question, pas question! Je ne vous laisserai pas entrer."

"Et bien je vais souffler, souffler, souffler...Je vais démolir ta maison."

Et il souffle très fort, souffle,

But le loup ne peut pas démolir la maison de briques

Poor, misérable loup, he had to go home très, très, très hungry.

🔊 **Turn the audio off.**

PERFORMANCE CHALLENGE:

There are four parts to this Performance Challenge:
1. Read the story silently to yourself.
2. Read the story aloud to yourself.
3. Read the story aloud to a parent, friend or one of your brothers and sisters.
4. Retell the story in your own words, using as much French as you can, to a parent, friend or one of your brothers or sisters. Don't worry if you can't remember every word. Do the best you can, and review the audio if you need to.

The Three Pigs II

(Story Telling)

Turn the audio on.

Lisa: Okay, so when it says la maison ne tombait pas, that means the house that would not fall. Right?

Tony: Right. And the house that would not fall in the story is the house made of brick.

Lisa: Yeah. So, the clue must be hidden under one of these bricks!

Narrator: Both of you, with the help of Madeleine and Michel, begin to look under the bricks scattered around. You turn over one brick, and underneath is a piece of parchment.

Lisa: Look at this! It looks like another puzzle. This one looks hard. Look, though, it looks like all of the words are from the story, *Les trois petits cochons*. Do you think that we remember enough of the story to solve the puzzle.

Tony: I think we do. I have an idea. Let's go through the story and try to tell it ourselves. We can help each other.

Lisa: That's a great idea!

Now retell the story in your own words, using as much French as possible. Use the pictures to remember the words you have learned.

Turn the audio off.

Word Puzzle 1

(The Three Pigs)

🔊 Turn the audio on.

Track 18

Tony: Okay. We've got that down pretty well. Let's take a look and see if this puzzle makes any sense.

🔊 Turn the audio off.

Fill in the blanks in the puzzle below by following the numbered clues. The letters that fall in the circled blanks will make an additional word that will help you on your adventure.

1. hunger
2.
3. brother
4. pig
5. walks
6. 🐷

1. 🐷
2. think

1. straw
2. 🏠

5 *Track 19*

🔊 Turn the audio on.

Lisa: "Marché à Aix." What does that mean?

Tony: Oh, no. We have to get back home! It's past time for us to go!

Lisa: Thank you, Michel.

Tony: Yeah, thanks.

Michel: You're welcome. Bonne chance.

🔈 Turn the audio off.

A Circus Act

(Horseshoe Story)

🔊))) **Turn the audio on.**

Track 20 **Narrator:** Tuesday, 10 a.m. Early this morning Madeleine takes you to Aix-en-Provence, a beautiful town outside of Avignon. You have come to the marché on market day, and the streets are swarming with people.

Lisa: Could this really be the right place? There's so many people here.

Tony: We're never going to be able to find anything in this crowd. What does Grandpa say in his notebook about where to find the next clue?

Lisa: Let me see. "The map I found led me to the marché in Aix-en-Provence." Oh, good! We're in the right place. "The next clue in the memoirs said that I must recherchez l'éléphant. I understood this to refer to the story of Un spectacle de cirque." Here, he tells the story.

Track 21

Un spectacle de cirque

1 Un éléphant se tient sur le plancher.

2 Un tigre saute sur le dos de l'éléphant.

3 Un chien saute sur le dos du tigre.

4 Un singe saute sur le dos du chien.

5 Un chat saute sur le dos du singe.

6 Soudain, une souris court à travers le plancher.

7 Le chat saute du dos du singe.

8 Le singe saute du dos du chien.

9 Le chien saute du dos du tigre.

10 Le tigre saute du dos de l'éléphant.

11 L'éléphant, le tigre, le chien, le singe, et le chat chassent la souris.

12 Mais la souris se sauve.

13 La souris a de la chance!

🔊 **Turn the audio off.**

PERFORMANCE CHALLENGE:

Create hand actions to represent the actions in the horseshoe story. (For example: Make up different actions to represent the animals you heard about in the story.) After you have created the actions, perform your mini-play for a parent, friend, or one of your bothers and sisters. Remember to narrate your actions in French and then translate your words if your audience does not understand French.

A Circus Act

(Match and Learn)

🔊 **Turn the audio on.**

Track 22

Tony: Éléphant. That means "elephant," doesn't it?

Lisa: Yeah. We should look for an elephant.

Tony: Well, that could be anything. It could be a statue, or a painting, or in a zoo...

Lisa: Hey, look! Isn't that Grandpa Glen's neighbor? The one with the bad name... Malien?

Tony: You're right! What is he doing here?

Madeleine: Oh, Malien. Je ne l'aime pas. I don't like him.

Lisa: I know. I don't want him to see us.

Narrator: Quickly all of you duck into an alley behind a booth.

Tony: Is he gone?

Lisa: No, he's still wandering around out there. It looks like he's searching for something.

Tony: I don't trust him. Hey, look at that! On the wall! There's a mural of an elephant.

Lisa: You're right! It's a good thing we hid in here, otherwise we would have never found it.

Tony: Well, look. A little farther down the mural is a picture of a tiger. Was there a tiger in the story? Let's look through the words we need to know for the story to check.

Practice your new French words by pointing to the pictures when you hear the words.

Track 23

1.

2.

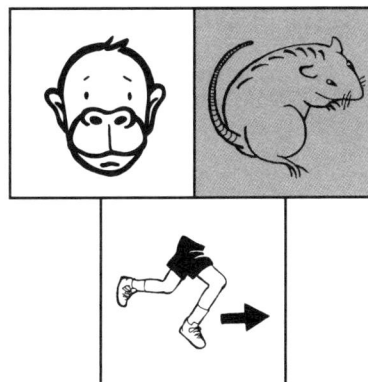

3.

4.

5.

6.

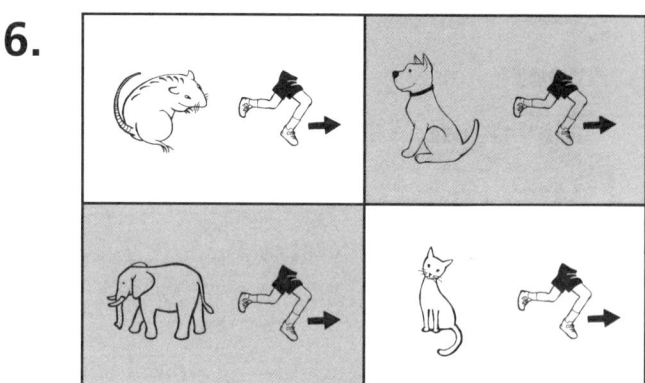

Track 24

Tony: Well, that's it then. Let's follow the animals back and see where it takes us.

Lisa: But Tony, it's almost three p.m. We have to go home soon.

Tony: I don't want to out into the market again. We might run into Malien. Come on, let's find the clue. We'll be quick.

Narrator: You begin to follow the trail of animals through the streets of Aix.

Turn the audio off.

PERFORMANCE CHALLENGE:

Draw a scene using the pictures you learned in your Match and Learn exercise. After you draw your picture, describe each part of the scene to a parent, friend, or one of your brothers or sisters. Remember to use as much French as you can to talk about your drawing.

A Circus Act

(Horseshoe Story Review)

🔊 **Turn the audio on.**

Track 25

Narrator: Tuesday, 3 p.m. You stand in front of an old house. You have followed the trail of animals here.

Lisa: What is this place?

Tony: Well, according to this sign, this is called the "Atelier de Cézanne."

Madeleine: Oui. Atelier means "workshop" and Cézanne was a very famous painter. He was born in Aix-en-Provence. This was where he painted.

Lisa: Cool.

Narrator: You go inside. The people who restored the atelier have left it just as if Cézanne was coming home at any minute, and you feel oddly as if you're in someone's private house.

Lisa: Look! There! There's a mouse painted on the wall!

Narrator: You all crowd around the painting. There is a mouse, and underneath it, in a crack in the wall, you find another puzzle folded up.

Lisa: It looks like it uses the words from *Un spectacle de cirque.* We should review the story and make sure we know it well enough to do the puzzle.

Track 26

Un spectacle de cirque

1 Un éléphant se tient sur le plancher.

2 Un tigre saute sur le dos de l'éléphant.

3 Un chien saute sur le dos du tigre.

4 Un singe saute sur le dos du chien.

5 Un chat saute sur le dos du singe.

6 Soudain, une souris court à travers le plancher.

7 Le chat saute du dos du singe.

8 Le singe saute du dos du chien.

9 Le chien saute du dos du tigre.

10 Le tigre saute du dos de l'éléphant.

11 L'éléphant, le tigre, le chien, le singe, et le chat chassent la souris.

12 Mais la souris se sauve.

13 La souris a de la chance!

🔊 **Turn the audio off.**

PERFORMANCE CHALLENGE:

Create hand actions to represent the actions in the horseshoe story. (For example: Make up different actions to represent the animals you heard about in the story.) After you have created the actions, perform your mini-play for a parent, friend, or one of your bothers and sisters. Remember to narrate your actions in French and then translate your words if your audience does not understand French.

Word Puzzle 2

(A Circus Act)

Track 27

🔊 Turn the audio on.

Tony: Okay, I think I know the story perfectly. Let's see if we can do the puzzle now.

🔊 Turn the audio off.

Fill in the blanks in the puzzle below by following the numbered clues. The letters that fall in the circled blanks will make an additional word that will help you on your adventure.

1.
2.
3.
4.
5.

1. back

2. floor

3. but

4.

5 *Track 28*

🔊))) **Turn the audio on.**

Lisa: "Notre-Dame." What do you think that means?

Madeleine: Notre-Dame is a famous cathédrale in Paris near where I live.

Tony: We're going to Paris? Cool!

Lisa: Well, first we'd better get home. Otherwise Mom and Dad will never let us go out again!

🔊 **Turn the audio off.**

Test 1

(Review)

🔊))) **Turn the audio on.**

Track 29

Narrator: As you drive home in the darkening evening, you look over the map of France that Madeleine has in her car.

Lisa: Look, Paris is all the way up here... do you think that Mom and Dad will let us go that far away?

Tony: I don't know. Madeleine, would you be willing to take us?

Madeleine: Oui. I need to go home soon anyway, chez moi.

Lisa: I don't think Mom and Dad are going to be very happy about this. We're already going to be home late.

Tony: Yeah, but think how much French we've learned!

Lisa: Hey, I've got an idea. Maybe if we show our parents how much French we know, they would let us go to Paris.

Tony: It's worth a try. We'd better practice before we get home.

Unit One Test

A. Frame Identifications

For each question, you will see a box with pictures. You will hear a statement about one of the pictures. There will be a pause of 10 seconds to identify the picture, and then the statement will be repeated.

Track 30

1.

2.

3.

4.

5.

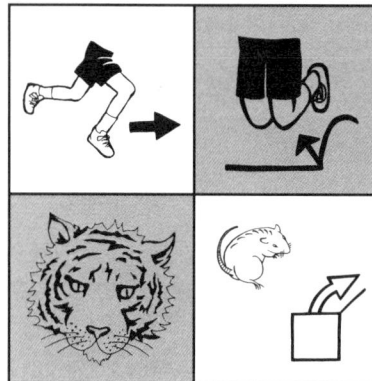

Comprehension Multiple-Choice

Track 31

Complete the following conversations by choosing the correct answer from the options listed.

1. *Comment ça va?*

    A. *Au revoir!*

    B. *Trés bien, merci.*

    C. *Bonjour.*

    D. *Dormez-vous.*

2. The little pig built his house out of *paille. C'est une bonne idée?*

    A. *Oui, le loup parle anglais.*

    B. *Oui, c'est une bonne idée.*

    C. *Non, ce n'est pas une bonne idée.*

    D. *Non, c'est planches.*

3. Who built his house out of *briques*?

    A. *le tigre*

    B. *le chien*

    C. *le cochon numéro trois*

    D. *le chat*

4. Who gets away from the circus act?

    A. *le souris*

    B. *le chat*

    C. *l'éléphant*

    D. *le cochon*

5. How would Tony introduce himself in French?

    A. *Je ne suis pas Tony.*

    B. *Mon frére est Tony.*

    C. *Je m'appelle Tony.*

    D. *Le petit cochon s'appelle Tony.*

Now go on to complete the reading/writing portion of this test.

◀ **Turn the audio off.**

Matching

Choose the statements that match and draw a line to connect the two.

1. wolf	A. *la maison*
2. straw	B. *le petit cochon*
3. house	C. *la maison de briques*
4. house of bricks	D. *le loup*
5. little pig	E. *la paille*

True or False

Write T or F for each statement.

_____ 1. *Le petit frére* built his *maison* out of *paille*.

_____ 2. *Le deuxiéme petit cochon* built his *maison* out of *bois*.

_____ 3. *Le loup démolit la maison de briques*.

_____ 4. *Le deuxiéme petit cochon démolit la maison de bois*.

_____ 5. *Le petit frére s'échappe et court á la maison le deuxéme petit cochon*.

Answer Key

1.

2.

3.

4.

5.

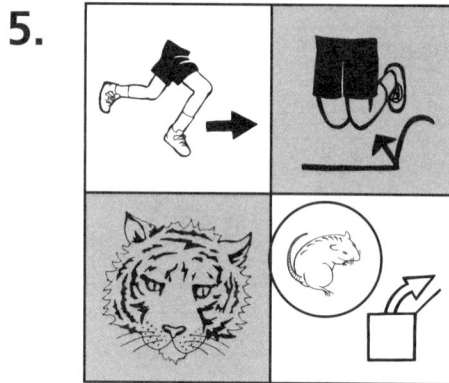

Comprehension Multiple-Choice

1. B. Trés bien, merci.

2. C. Non, ce n'est pas une bonne idée.

3. C. le cochon numéro trois

4. A. le souris

5. C. Je m'appelle Tony.

Matching

1. D

2. E

3. A

4. C

5. B

True or False

1. T

2. T

3. F

4. F

5. T

Alouette

(Ditties)

🔊 Turn the audio on.

Narrator: Wednesday, 10 a.m. Having impressed your parents your new French skills, they agree to let Madeleine take you with her to Paris. You leave early in the morning when the sun is just coming up and the sky is still gray, in order to arrive in Paris before 10 a.m. You go directly to the Notre-Dame Cathedral.

Lisa: Look, Tony, there's a sign here. It says, "This cathedral was originally built in the twelfth century by Maurice de Sully." Wow. That's really old.

Tony: Yeah. It's neat looking too, with all that stone and those windows.

Lisa: Should we go inside?

Tony: Sure. We have to find the clue.

Narrator: You enter into the huge, silent cathedral. It is dark on the inside, with candles burning, throwing shadows.

Lisa: This place is huge. We're never going to be able to find anything in here.

Narrator: You both begin to search the cathedral. It is full of small alcoves and cloisters, and you eventually become discouraged.

Tony: I don't even know what we're looking for.

Lisa: Well, let's look at the notebook.

Tony: Okay. Hey! Look here, Grandpa wrote down the words to "Alouette." I remember that song.

Lisa: It must be a clue. Let's sing it through and see if it helps us.

Tony: Okay. I'll go first.

Alouette, gentille alouette,

Alouette, je te plumerai.

Je te plumerai la tête,

Je te plumerai la tête.

Et la tête, et la tête,

Alouette, Alouette, oh!

Alouette, gentille alouette,

Alouette, je te plumerai.

Lisa: I'll go next.

Alouette, gentille alouette,

Alouette, je te plumerai.

Je te plumerai le bec,

Je te plumerai le bec.

Et le bec, et le bec,

Et la tête, et la tête,

Alouette, Alouette, oh!

Alouette, gentille alouette,

Alouette, je te plumerai.

Tony & Lisa:

Alouette, gentille alouette,

Alouette, je te plumerai.

Je te plumerai les pattes,

Je te plumerai les pattes.

Et les pattes, et les pattes,

Et le bec, et le bec,

Et la tête, et la tête,

Alouette, Alouette, oh!

Alouette, gentille alouette,

Alouette, je te plumerai.

Tony:

Alouette, gentille alouette,

Alouette, je te plumerai.

Je te plumerai les ailes,

Je te plumerai les ailes.

Et les pattes, et les pattes,

Et le bec, et le bec,

Et la tête, et la tête,

Alouette, Alouette, oh!

Alouette, gentille alouette,

Alouette, je te plumerai.

Lisa:

Alouette, gentille alouette,

Alouette, je te plumerai.

Je te plumerai le dos,

Je te plumerai le dos.

Et le dos, et le dos,

Et les ailes, et les ailes,

Et les pattes, et les pattes,

Et le bec, et le bec,

Et la tête, et la tête,

Alouette, Alouette, oh!

Alouette, gentille alouette,

Alouette, je te plumerai.

Tony & Lisa:

Alouette, gentille alouette,

Alouette, je te plumerai.

Je te plumerai la queue,

Je te plumerai la queue.

Et la queue, et la queue,

Et le dos, et le dos,

Et les ailes, et les ailes,

Et les pattes, et les pattes,

Et le bec, et le bec,

Et la tête, et la tête,

Alouette, Alouette, oh!

Alouette, gentille alouette,

Alouette, je te plumerai.

Lisa: Good job. I'm not sure I know what it has to do with the clue, though.

Madeleine: It's getting late. We need to leave. We can find the clue tomorrow.

🔈 **Turn the audio off.**

PERFORMANCE CHALLENGE:

Now that you have learned a new song, share your French with a parent, friend, or one of your brothers or sisters by teaching them the song. Remember to teach it in French and then translate the words into English if your partner does not understand French.

Une Souris Verte

(Ditties)

🔊 Turn the audio on.

Track 2 **Narrator:** Madeleine introduces you to her parents, who seem pleased to meet you. They feed you an enormous dinner, including ratatouille. If you would like to try to make ratatouille, there is a recipe in the back of your workbook. After dinner, you sit down in the living room to take a closer look at the notebook to see if you can find any clues.

Lisa: Look, Tony, there's another song here. And see, Grandpa wrote a riddle underneath.

Tony: What does it say?

Lisa: It says, "Je suis dans la tête de la souris." Remember the word souris from the Circus Act song? Souris means mouse. What do you think the rest of it means?

Tony: Well...look here. Grandpa wrote down another song. It also has the word "souris" in it. We must need to know the song in order to find the clue.

Lisa: You're right. Let's take a look. I think I remember hearing Grandpa sing this song. It goes like this:

> Une souris verte
>
> Qui courait dans l'herbe
>
> Je l'attrape par la queue
>
> Je la montre à ces messieurs
>
> Ces messieurs me disent
>
> Trempez là dans l'huile,
>
> Trempez là dans l'eau.
>
> Ça fera un escargot tout chaud.
>
> Je la mets dans un tiroir
>
> Elle me dit il fait trop noir.
>
> Je la mets dans mon chapeau
>
> Elle me dit il fait trop chaud.

Tony: That's cool. Let me try.

> Une souris verte
>
> Qui courait dans l'herbe
>
> Je l'attrape par la queue

Je la montre à ces messieurs

Ces messieurs me disent

Trempez là dans l'huile,

Trempez là dans l'eau.

Ça fera un escargot tout chaud.

Je la mets dans un tiroir

Elle me dit il fait trop noir.

Je la mets dans mon chapeau

Elle me dit il fait trop chaud.

Lisa: Good. Let's sing it together.

Tony & Lisa:

Une souris verte

Qui courait dans l'herbe

Je l'attrape par la queue

Je la montre à ces messieurs

Ces messieurs me disent

Trempez là dans l'huile,

Trempez là dans l'eau.

Ça fera un escargot tout chaud.

Je la mets dans un tiroir

Elle me dit il fait trop noir.

Je la mets dans mon chapeau

Elle me dit il fait trop chaud.

Tony: Great! Let's see if we can figure out that clue now.

🔊 **Turn the audio off.**

PERFORMANCE CHALLENGE:

Now that you have learned a new song, share your French with a parent, friend, or one of your brothers or sisters by teaching them the song. Remember to teach it in French and then translate the words into English if your partner does not understand French.

Chicken Little I

(Scatter Chart)

Turn the audio on.

Narrator: Wednesday, 6 p.m. It's raining outside now and you are both stuck inside Madeleine's house until it stops. You are frustrated because you want to go back to the cathedral to look for the clue. Madeleine has gone out to buy some groceries.

Tony: I guess it doesn't really matter because we wouldn't even know where to look.

Lisa: Hey, Tony! See here... it looks like Grandpa drew something in the notebook.

Tony: What is it? It just looks like scribbles.

Lisa: Do you remember the riddle? "Je suis dans la tête de la souris"

Tony: Yeah... hey, I see what you mean. It kind of looks like a mouse, a souris. But what are all of these other signs?

Lisa: Well, I think it might be a map of the Notre-Dame Cathedral. See? This is where we came in, here.

Tony: You know, I think you're right. If the riddle is hidden in the tête, then...

Lisa: It would be right here!

Tony: We've got to get back there, fast!

Lisa: How? It's raining outside, and Madeleine is still at the store.

Tony: I guess we'll have to wait then. It makes me nervous, though. I'm sure that someone else is after that treasure. Do you know who I think it is?

Lisa: Who?

Tony: That neighbor of Grandpa Glen's...what was his name? Malien?

Lisa: You might be right. But there's nothing we can do about it now. Hey, I've got an idea. Let's check the notebook and see if there's anything else we need to learn in order to find the clue.

Tony: Good idea. Let's see. Yeah... "In order to figure out the next clue I had to learn a new story in French called 'Le ciel tombe.'" This might be hard. It has a lot of new words in it.

Lisa: That's okay. Let's go through them until Madeleine gets back.

Look at the pictures on your workbook page and point to what you hear.

la taniére
the cave

la tête
the head

l'oie
the goose

les yeux
the eyes

le morceau
piece

la dinde
the turkey

le ciel
the sky

le renard
the fox

la poule
the hen

les animaux
the animals

la feuille
the leaf

le poussin
the chickie

le canard
the duck

🔊 **Turn the audio off.**

PERFORMANCE CHALLENGE:

Choose five of the new words and pictures that you learned in the Scatter Chart. Show the pictures to a parent, friend, or one of your brothers or sisters and explain to them how you think the picture represents the words you have learned.

Chicken Little I

(Match and Learn)

))) Turn the audio on.

Narrator: You don't have to wait long for Madeleine to return. She is skeptical about going back to the cathedral now that it's dark, but she finally agrees. Trembling with excitement, you take a flashlight and head out the door. Once outside, you both run through the rain to Madeleine's car. The car isn't very far away, but your shoes and ankles are covered with mud by the time you get there. It only takes a few minutes to arrive at the cathedral. You all sit in the car.

Lisa: It's kind of spooky here in the dark.

Tony: Too late to turn back now.

Narrator: Finally, you follow Madeleine and run through the rain into the Cathedral, which is groaning slightly in the wind. You turn on your flashlight and creep along the stone wall.

Tony: Okay. According to Grandpa Glen's map, there should be a small alcove up here on the left.

Narrator: You all sneak along quietly, and after double checking the map, you find a small alcove you missed before.

Lisa: This must be it.

Tony: It looks kind of scary. What if there are bats or something inside?

Lisa: There's nothing inside except a clue. Do you think we know enough of the story to figure it out?

Tony: I don't know. There's still new words to learn.

Lisa: Well, let's take a look at them.

Practice your new French words by pointing to the pictures when you hear the words.

1.

2.

3.

4.

5.

6.

7.

8.

🔊 **Turn the audio off.**

PERFORMANCE CHALLENGE:

Draw a scene using the pictures you learned in your Match and Learn exercise. After you draw your picture, describe each part of the scene to a parent, friend, or one of your brothers or sisters. Remember to use as much French as you can to talk about your drawing.

Chicken Little I

(Diglot Weave)

🔊)) **Turn the audio on.**

Track 7

Narrator: You all squeeze into the alcove and begin to look for the clue.

Tony: Hey. What's this?

Lisa: It looks like a note. It has writing on it. It says, "Le ciel tombe." Madeleine, what does that mean?

Madeleine: I don't know how to say it in English.

Tony: That's okay. Isn't it in the story?

Lisa: Maybe. Let's go through the story and see if we can figure out what it means.

This is the story of a poussin that convinced itself that le ciel was falling. One day this poussin was in the garden when une feuille, a big feuille, fell on her tête.

Track 8

The poor poussin was startled and imagined that le ciel was falling. It started to run, screaming, "Peep, peep, Mommy, where are you, Mommy?"

"Cluck, cluck, here I am, Poussin. What is it?"

"Le ciel is falling! Le ciel is falling!"

"How do you know, Poussin?"

"I saw it with my very yeux and un morceau of it fell on my tête. I tell you the truth."

"Let's flee!" screamed la poule. "Let's flee, run! Canard, Canard, where are you, Canard?"

"Quack, quack, here I am. What happened, what happened?"

"Le ciel is falling! Le ciel is falling!"

"How do you know, Poule?"

"Poussin told me."

"How do you know, Poussin?"

"I saw it with my very yeux, and un morceau of it fell on my tête. I tell you the truth."

"Well, let's flee!" screamed Canard. "Let's flee, run! Oie, oie, where are you, Oie?"

"Honk, honk, here I am, Canard. What happened?"

"Le ciel is falling! Le ciel is falling!"

"How do you know, Canard?"

"Poule told me."

"How do you know, Poule?"

"Poussin told me."

"How do you know, Poussin?"

"I saw it with my very yeux and un morceau of it fell on my tête. I tell you the truth."

"Oh, let's flee!" screamed Oie, "Let's flee, run! Dinde, Dinde, where are you, Dinde?"

"Gobble, gobble, here I am, Oie. What happened?"

"Le ciel is falling! Le ciel is falling!"

"How do you know, Oie?"

"Canard told me."

"How do you know Canard?"

"Poule told me."

"How do you know, Poule?"

"Poussin told me."

"How do you know, Poussin?"

" Oh, I saw it with my very yeux, and un morceau of it fell on my tête. I tell you the truth."

"Well, let's flee!" screamed Dinde. "Let's flee, run! Renard, Renard, where are you, Renard?"

"Yif, yif. Here I am. What happened?"

"Le ciel is falling! Le ciel is falling!"

"How do you know, Dinde?"

"Oie told me."

"How do know, Oie?"

"Canard told me."

"How do you know, Canard."

"Poule told me."

"How do you know, Poule?"

"Poussin told me."

"How do you know, Poussin?"

"I saw it with my very yeux, and un morceau of it fell on my tête. I tell you the truth."

Renard thought a little and said, "Don't be afraid. I'll save you. Come with me to my tanière."

And all the animaux went with the Renard into her tanière. But la dinde et l'oie et le canard et la poule et le poussin never came out. Le renard ate them all.

You see a false rumor can lead to tragedy.

🔊 **Turn the audio off.**

PERFORMANCE CHALLENGE:

There are four parts to this Performance Challenge:
1. Read the story silently to yourself.
2. Read the story aloud to yourself.
3. Read the story aloud to a parent, friend or one of your brothers and sisters.
4. Retell the story in your own words, using as much French as you can, to a parent, friend or one of your brothers or sisters. Don't worry if you can't remember every word. Do the best you can, and review the audio if you need to.

Chicken Little I

(Review Questions)

🔊 Turn the audio on.

Track 9

Tony: What do we need to look for?

Narrator: Suddenly the batteries in the flashlight run out and you are plunged into darkness.

Madeleine: Calmez-vous. It's okay. Stay here, I'll go get another flashlight from my car.

Narrator: Madeleine leaves, and you both sit trembling in the dark.

Lisa: What can we do until she gets back? Tony . . . I'm scared.

Tony: I know. I am too. Let's just keep talking. Maybe we can review what we know about the story. Madeleine will be back soon. I promise.

Lisa: Yeah, you're right. Okay. Let's ask each other questions about the story. Do you think you remember it enough?

Note: Review questions are audio only.

🔊 Turn the audio off.

Chicken Little II

(Scatter Chart)

🔊 **Turn the audio on.**

Track 10

Narrator: Wednesday, 8 p.m. You sit frightened in the dark cathedral, the wind howling outside.

Tony: Shhh. I hear something.

Malien: Est ce que j'ai entendu quelque chose?

Lisa: Doesn't that sound like Grandpa's neighbor, Malien?

Tony: Shh!

Malien: J'espère que ces gosses ne soient pas ici. Ils ruinent mes projets.

Tony: Do you believe me now? Why else would Malien be here if he isn't trying to stop us from helping Grandpa Glen?

Malien: Je ne pense pas qu'ils sont ici. Je devrais partir.

Lisa: Is he gone?

Tony: I'm not sure. Let's wait a second.

Lisa: I think he's gone.

Tony: It feels like we've been in this cathedral forever. We'll never know that story well enough to solve the puzzle.

Lisa: Sure we will. We are understanding more and more each time we go over it. There are just a few more words to understand before we get it all.

Track 11

Look at the boxes on your workbook page and point to what you hear...

il(elle) me l'a dit *he (she) told me*	**Comment tu le sais?** *how do you know it?*	**Je suis ici** *here I am*	**venez avec moi** *you all come with me*
tombe *it is falling*	**Oú es-tu?** *where are you?*	**Je te dis la vérité** *I am telling you the truth*	**Je l'ai vu** *I saw it*

🔊 **Turn the audio off.**

PERFORMANCE CHALLENGE:

Choose several of the words and phrases that you learned in the Scatter Chart. Write as many sentences as you can using these words and phrases (and others that you already know). If you want to, create your own story with the sentences. Read the sentences that you create to a parent, friend, or one of your brothers or sisters. Remember to translate the French if your partner does not understand French.

Chicken Little II

(Match and Learn)

6
Track 12

◀))) **Turn the audio on.**

Narrator: In the cathedral, 8:30 p.m. You hear footsteps.

Tony: Shh! Malien might be coming back.

Madeleine: Les enfants! Est-ce que vous êtes toujours ici?

Lisa: It's Madeleine! Madeleine! Madeleine, we're in here!

Narrator: Madeleine brings a flashlight, and takes you back to her house. In no time she and her parents have tucked you into bed.

Lisa: Tony? Do you think we'll be able to find Grandpa Glen tomorrow?

Tony: I hope so. We need to go back and find that clue. Then we'll just have to go from there.

Lisa: I don't think I'll be able to sleep. I'm too scared. I can't believe that Malien followed us to the cathedral.

Tony: I know. It frightens me too. I'm also scared that I won't know enough French to figure out the next clue.

Lisa: I've got an idea. Let's go over the last few things we need to know for the story.

Tony: What a good idea! I'm not tired, anyway.

6
Track 13

Practice your new French words by pointing to what you hear.

1.

Where are you?	here I am
I saw it	it is falling

2.

Where are you, Hen?	I saw it
the sky is falling	Here I am, Chickie

3.

How do you know it?	the chickie told it to me
I am telling you the truth	you all come with me

4.

the animals run	Where are you, Goose?
Here I am, Hen	the sky is falling

5.

How do you know it, Hen?	I saw it
the chickie told it to me	How do you know it, Chickie?

6.

I am telling you the truth	you all come with me
The chick sees the turkey.	the animals run

7.

hen told it to me	How do you know it, Hen?
the sky is falling	How do you know it, Goose?

8.

you all come with me	the animals and the cave
the animals run	the chickie sees the fox

◁)) **Turn the audio off.**

PERFORMANCE CHALLENGE:

List all the names of the animals from this activity in French and English and teach them to a parent, friend, or one of your brothers or sisters.

Chicken Little II

(Diglot Weave)

Track 14

🔊)) **Turn the audio on.**

Narrator: You can barely wait for Madeleine to wake up the next morning. As soon as she is up you begin begging her to let you go back to the cathedral. She agrees, and you all walk back together. The air is clean and fresh after last night's rain. Once again you enter the cathedral and find the small alcove of the night before. It isn't scary at all in the daylight.

Tony: Okay. Now, the clue says, "Le ciel tombe." Right? That's in the story, I remember, but we need to figure out what it means.

Lisa: Yeah. Let's go through the story one more time.

Track 15

Le ciel tombe! Le ciel tombe!

This is the 📖 *of a little* 🐤 *that convinced itself that* ☁ *was falling.*

One day... Un jour this 🐤 *was in the garden when une* 🍃 *, une grande* 🍃 *,*

Fell on her 👤 *. The poor* 🐤 *was startled and imagined that* ☁

was falling. It started to à courir, screaming: "Peep, peep, Mommy, mommy, where are

you? Maman,

Maman, où es-tu Maman?"

"Cluck, cluck, here I am, 🐤 *...je suis ici. What happened? Qu'est-ce qu'il y a?"*

" ☁ *is falling!...* ☁ ⌐ *!"*

"How do you know...comment tu le sais?"

"I saw it with my very 👁 👁, Maman...I saw it avec mes 👁 👁. Un ▽ of sky fell on

my 😊 . I tell you the truth."

"Let's flee!" screamed 🐔 . "Let's flee. Run! Duck, Duck, where are you...où es-tu,

🦆 ?"

"Quack, quack, here I am... je suis ici. Qu'est-ce qui se passe?"

" ☁☀ 𝄆 , ☁☀ 𝄆 !"

"Huh? How do you know, 🐔 ...comment tu le sais?

" 🐤 told me so... 🐤 me l'a dit."

"Comment tu le sais, 🐤 ?"

"I saw it avec mes 👁 👁. Un ▽ de ☁☀ est 𝄆 on my 😊 . I tell you the

truth...Je te dis la vérité."

"Let's flee! Run!" a crié 🦆 . "Allons nous-en, courous...Run! Goose, Goose, où es-

tu, 🦢 ?"

"Honk, honk, je suis ici, 🦆 . Qu'est-ce qui se passe?"

" ☁☀ 𝄆 , ☁☀ 𝄆 !"

"Huh, comment tu le sais, ?"

" told me so... me l'a dit."

"Comment tu le sais, ?"

" me l'a dit."

"Comment tu le sais, ?"

"I saw it avec mes . Un de est sur ma . I tell you the

truth...Je te dis la vérité."

"Let's flee!" a crié l'oie. "Allons nous-en! Turkey, turkey, où es-tu, ?"

"Gobble, gobble, je suis ici, . Qu'est-ce qui se passe?"

" , !"

"Huh, comment tu le sais, ?"

" me l'a dit."

"Comment tu le sais, ?"

" me l'a dit."

"Comment tu le sais, ?"

"Le *me l'a dit."*

"Comment tu le sais, *."*

"I saw it...Je l'ai vu de mes *et un* *de ciel est* *sur ma* *. Je te dis la vérité."*

"Allons nous-en!" a crié *. "Allons nous-en, courons! Fox, Fox, where are you,* *?"*

"Yif, yif. Je suis ici. Qu'est-ce qui se passe?"

" *,* *!"*

"Ohhh. Comment tu le sais, *?"*

"L'oie me l'a dit."

"Comment tu le sais, *?"*

" *me l'a dit."*

"Comment tu le sais, *?"*

" *me l'a dit."*

"Comment tu le sais, *?"*

"Le *me l'a dit."*

"Comment tu le sais, *?"*

"Je l'ai vu de mes 👁 👁 *. Un* ▽ *de ciel est* ↯⌐ *sur ma* 🙂 *. Je te dis la vérité."*

thought a little, and then calmly dit: "Don't be afraid. N'ayez pas peur. I'll save you all. Come with me, all of you...Venez avec moi. Venez avec moi dans ma tanière."

Then 🦃 *et* 🦢 *et* 🦆 *et* 🐔 *et le little* 🐤 *went avec* 🦊 *into her* *. What happened after that no one sait for sure. We only know that* 🦃 *et* 🦢 *, et* 🦆 *et* 🐔 *et le little* 🐤 *never came out de* *. What do you think happened to them dans* *? Do you think...penses-tu que* 🦊 *killed them and ate them all?*

That's what I think. I think 🦊 *les a tous mangés.*

Poor things.

🔊 **Turn the audio off.**

PERFORMANCE CHALLENGE:

There are four parts to this Performance Challenge:
1. Read the story silently to yourself.
2. Read the story aloud to yourself.
3. Read the story aloud to a parent, friend or one of your brothers and sisters.
4. Retell the story in your own words, using as much French as you can, to a parent, friend or one of your brothers or sisters. Don't worry if you can't remember every word. Do the best you can, and review the audio if you need to.

Chicken Little II

(Story Telling)

🔊 **Turn the audio on.**

Track 16

Tony: Okay. "Le ciel tombe" means "the sky is falling." Right?

Lisa: Right. So, how does that apply to the situation?

Tony: I'm not sure.

Lisa: I know. Let's tell the story to each other again, using as much French as we can remember. That really helped me last time.

Retell the story in your own words, using as much French as possible. Use the pictures to remember the words you have learned.

Track 17

Note: pause the audio while you tell the story

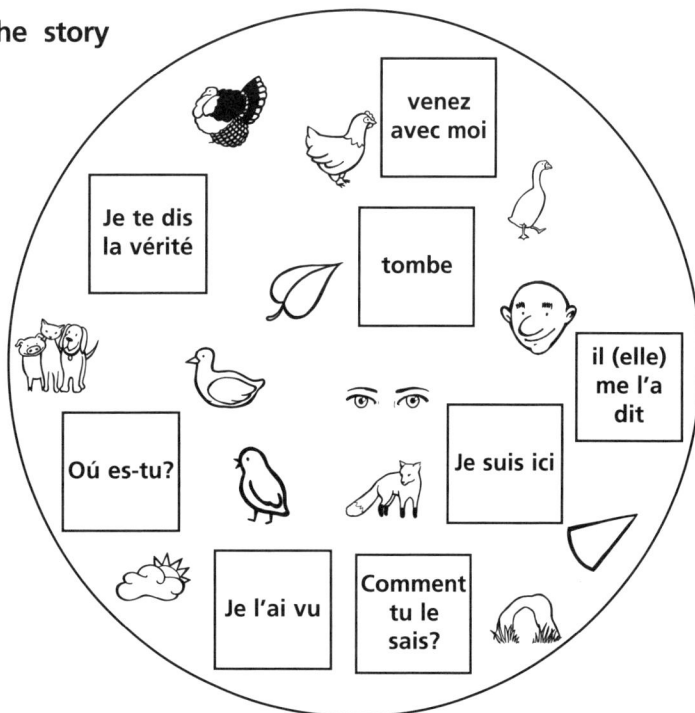

venez avec moi

Je te dis la vérité

tombe

il (elle) me l'a dit

Oú es-tu?

Je suis ici

Je l'ai vu

Comment tu le sais?

Tony: Okay. That gave me an idea. When le poussin thought that the sky was falling, it was really a leaf from above her head.

Lisa: Yeah... it would make sense if the clue was above our heads!

Narrator: You both look above you and see a small ledge. It's a stretch, but you manage to reach up and retrieve a piece of parchment.

Tony: We found it! We found the next clue!

🔊 **Turn the audio off.**

Word Puzzle 3

(Chicken Little)

Turn the audio on.

6
Track 18

Tony: It looks like a puzzle. We need the words from le poussin.

Lisa: Let's hurry up and do it. We don't have much time left to find Grandpa Glen.

Fill in the blanks in the puzzle below by following the numbered clues. The letters that fall in the circled blanks will make additional words that will help you on your adventure.

1.
2.
3.

1.
2. **truth**

1.
2.
3.
4.
5. **falling**
6.
8.

Turn the audio off.

6

Track 19

🔊))) Turn the audio on.

Tony: I don't know what "Arc de Triomphe" is. What's that there, on the bottom of the sheet?

Lisa: It looks like another riddle. It says, "Derrière le serpent est l'indice final."

Tony: Great. What does that mean?

🔊 Turn the audio off.

The Mantis and The Butterfly

(Horseshoe Story)

🔊 **Turn the audio on.**

Track 20

Lisa: I don't know. Do you suppose that this clue, "Arc de Triomphe," might lead us to the last clue?

Tony: I hope so.

Narrator: You both run back to Madeleine's house, and she agrees to take you to the Arc de Triomphe. It is an enormous arch, over 150 feet high, which the French Emperor Napoleon built in 1806. You stare at the massive structure while the Paris traffic buzzes around you.

Lisa: What now?

Tony: Well, it looks like Grandpa made a note in the journal. It says, "Having found the riddle that led to the last clue, I once again had to fall back on my knowledge of folklore. This riddle referred to an odd little story called 'La mante et le papillon.'"

La mante et le papillon

1 Ici, il y a une maison.
2 Et ici, il y a un jardin.
3 Dans le jardin, il y a un arbre.
4 Sur l'arbre, il y a une feuille.
5 Sur la feuille, il y a un papillon.
6 Derrière le papillon, il y a une mante.
7 Derrière la mante, il y a un oiseau.
8 Derrière l'oiseau, il y a un chat.
9 Derrière le chat, il y a un serpent.

10 Le serpent veut manger le chat.
11 Le chat veut manger l'oiseau.
12 L'oiseau veut manger la mante.
13 La mante veut manger le papillon.

14 Alors que se passe-t-il?
15 Le papillon voit la mante et s'envole.
16 La mante perd son repas.
17 L'oiseau vole vers une autre branche.
18 Le chat saute de l'arbre.
19 Le serpent rampe au loin.
20 Je suis content que le papillon ait vu la mante.

Track 21

🔊 **Turn the audio off.**

PERFORMANCE CHALLENGE:

Create hand actions to represent the actions in the horseshoe story. (For example: Make up different actions to represent the animals you heard about in the story.) After you have created the actions, perform your mini-play for a parent, friend, or one of your bothers or sisters. Remember to narrate your actions in French and then translate your words if your audience does not understand French.

The Mantis and The Butterfly

(Match and Learn)

Turn the audio on.

Track 22

Lisa: I don't know what that story means, really. I only understood some of the words.

Tony: Madeleine, can you help us learn the new words? Otherwise, we'll never find the next clue, or Grandpa Glen!

Madeleine: Of course. Listen carefully.

Practice some new French vocabulary by pointing to the pictures as you hear the words.

Track 23

1.

2.

3.

4.

5.

6.

🔊 **Turn the audio off.**

PERFORMANCE CHALLENGE:

Draw a scene using the pictures you learned in your Match and Learn exercise. After you draw your picture, describe each part of the scene to a parent, friend, or one of your brothers or sisters. Remember to use as much French as you can to talk about your drawing.

The Mantis and The Butterfly

(Horseshoe Story Review)

🔊 **Turn the audio on.**

6 *Track 24*

Narrator: Thursday, 10 a.m.
Lisa: Okay, we need to find a serpent, because the clue should be behind it. Right? "Derrière le serpent est l'indice final."
Tony: Where are we going to find le serpent around here?
Lisa: Well, it must be somewhere. Is there anything from the story that we're not understanding?
Tony: Maybe we should go through it one more time together—just to make sure.
Lisa: That's a good idea.

La mante et le papillon

6 *Track 25*

1 *Ici, il y a une maison.*
2 *Et ici, il y a un jardin.*
3 *Dans le jardin, il y a un arbre.*
4 *Sur l'arbre, il y a une feuille.*
5 *Sur la feuille, il y a un papillon.*
6 *Derrière le papillon, il y a une mante.*
7 *Derrière la mante, il y a un oiseau.*
8 *Derrière l'oiseau, il y a un chat.*
9 *Derrière le chat, il y a un serpent.*

10 *Le serpent veut manger le chat.*
11 *Le chat veut manger l'oiseau.*
12 *L'oiseau veut manger la mante.*
13 *La mante veut manger le papillon.*

14 *Alors que se passe-t-il ?*
15 *Le papillon voit la mante et s'envole.*
16 *La mante perd son repas.*
17 *L'oiseau vole vers une autre branche.*
18 *Le chat saute de l'arbre.*
19 *Le serpent rampe.au loin.*
20 *Je suis content que le papillon a vu la mante.*

🔊 **Turn the audio off.**

PERFORMANCE CHALLENGE:

Create hand actions to represent the actions in the horseshoe story. (For example: Make up different actions to represent the animals you heard about in the story.) After you have created the actions, perform your mini-play for a parent, friend, or one of your bothers or sisters. Remember to narrate your actions in French and then translate your words if your audience does not understand French.

Word Puzzle 4

(The Mantis and The Butterfly)

🔊 **Turn the audio on.**

Lisa: Hey, look. If you look closely at the Arc de Triomphe, there are designs and flowers engraved on the stone. I bet if we look hard enough, there would be a serpent.

Tony: I bet you're right! Come on, let's look!

Narrator: Quickly, the three of you begin to search the Arc.

Lisa: Look! Look! There's a serpent right here. And there's a space behind it.

Tony: Is there a clue?

Lisa: Let me see... yes, there is! It's another puzzle! We need the words from La mante et le papillon.

Fill in the blanks in the puzzle below by following the numbered clues. The letters that fall in the circled blanks will make an additional word that will help you on your adventure.

1. 🌸

2. 🌳

1. **to eat**

2. 🏠

3. 🍃

4. 🦋

5. **fly away**

6. 🦗

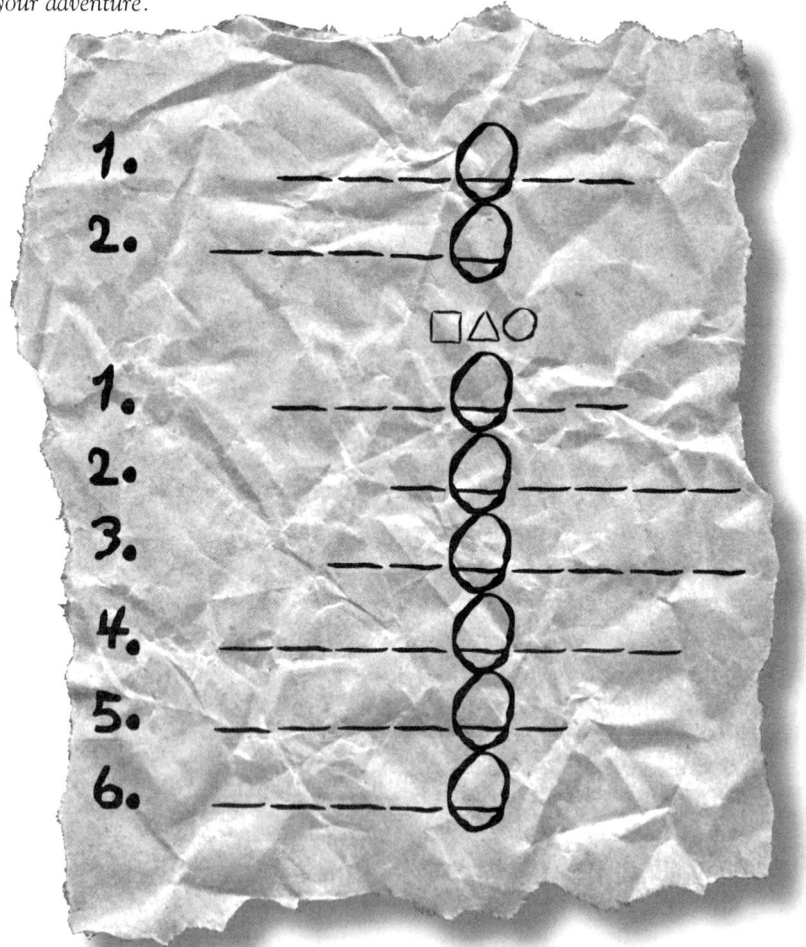

🔉 **Turn the audio off.**

6
Track 27

((•))) Turn the audio on.

Tony: Okay. It spells "De Gaulle."

Lisa: We should go back to Madeleine's house and call mom and dad. I think they should know what we've found so far.

◁ Turn the audio off.

Final Word Puzzle

(The Hidden Clue)

6
Track 28

)))) Turn the audio on.

Narrator: Tuesday, 11 a.m. You arrive at Madeleine's house, and you take out all of the puzzles you have done so far.

Tony: Okay, what now?

Lisa: What about this puzzle, the one that Grandpa Glen sent to us? Look, do you see these shapes next to each line? There are shapes like that in all of the answers to the other puzzles (see pages 33, 41, 75, and 82). I bet if we put those words into Grandpa's puzzle, we could figure out what to do.

Tony: Well, let's give it a try.

Turn the audio off.

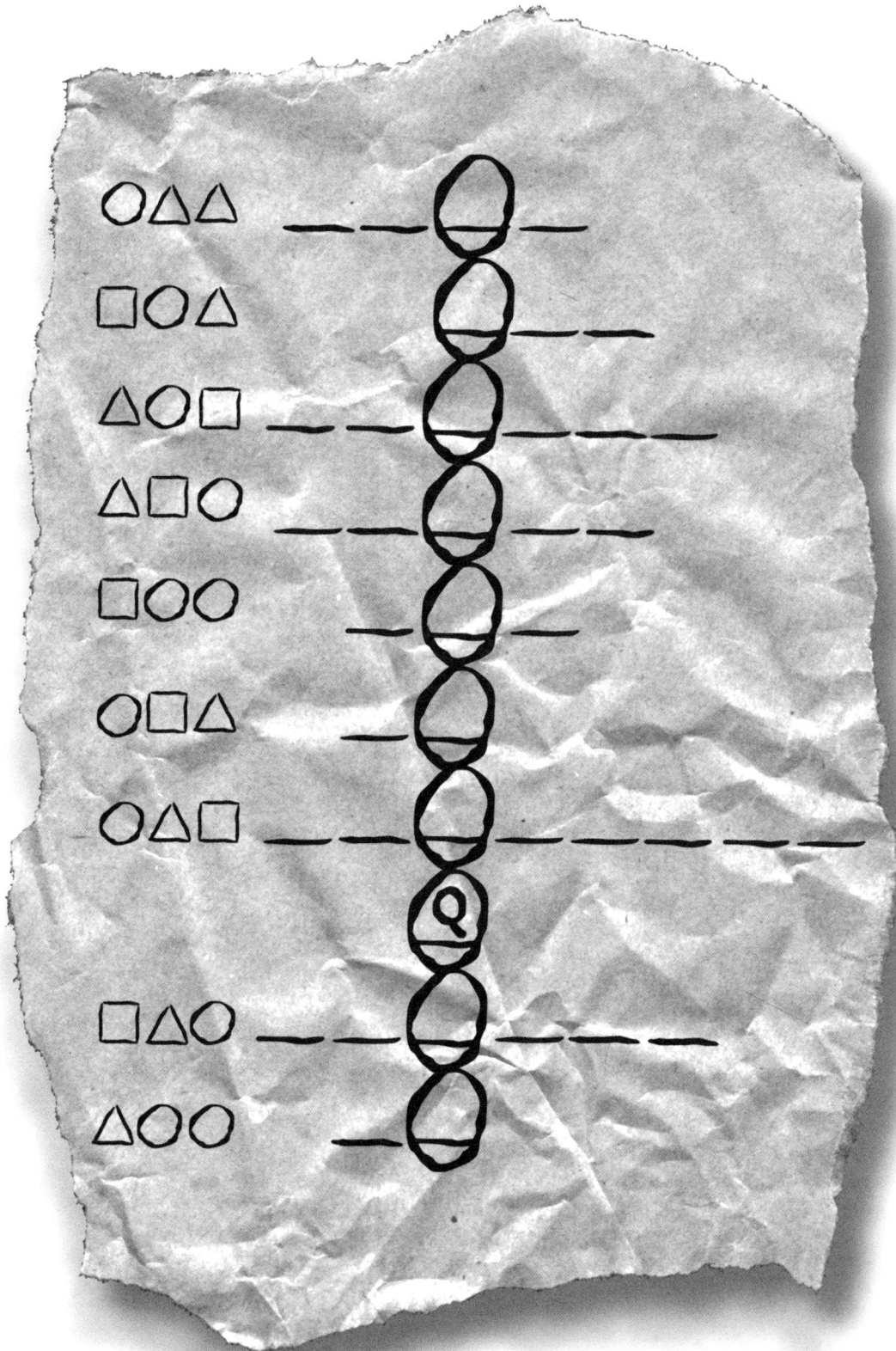

○△△   _ _ _ _ _

□○△   _ _ _

△○□   _ _ _ _ _

△□○   _ _ _ _

□○○   _ _ _

○□△   _ _

○△□   _ _ _ _ _ _ _

□△○   _ _ _ _ _ _ _

△○○   _ _

🔊))) Turn the audio on.

Lisa: So, what does "Martinique" mean?

Tony: I don't know. Let's look on the map.

Lisa: I don't see Martinique, but look! De Gaulle is the name of the airport! Grandpa must be at the airport! We have to go now!

🔊 Turn the audio off.

Grandpa!

(*The Reunion*)

Turn the audio on.

6
Track 30

Narrator: You are trying to convince Madeleine to take you to the airport. Right in the middle of your conversation there is a knock at the door. It's your parents! Concerned by how long you have been gone, they have come to get you. You tell them everything that has happened. Your parents are excited because they hadn't had any luck in finding your Grandpa. They agree to take you to the airport. When you arrive, you run ahead of your parents to the international gates. Guess who was waiting there for you?

Grandpa Glen: Hello, children. I was afraid that you wouldn't make it.

Lisa: Grandpa Glen! I'm so glad we found you!

Tony: Where is Martinique? Are you going there?

Lisa: Can we come with you?

Grandpa Glen: Of course, of course you can come with me. I bought two extra tickets. Martinique is a small island in the Caribbean and I have reason to believe the paintings are there. We must leave right away. We can't let Malien find the paintings first.

Narrator: Right then your parents catch up to you. Once they hear what Grandpa Glen is proposing they immediately object. They aren't exactly sure what is going on, but whatever it is they are afraid it will be too dangerous for children.

Tony: But, Mom, Dad! We've learned so much!

Lisa: Yes, and our French has gotten so much better!

Narrator: After exchanging looks, your mother and father say that if you can really prove how much French you've learned they'll let you go to Martinique with Grandpa. You take a deep breath.

Turn the audio off.

Test 2

(Review)

6
Track 31

🔊))) **Turn the audio on.**

A. Frame Identifications

For each question, you will see a box with pictures. You will hear a statement about one of the pictures. There will be a pause of 10 seconds to identify the picture, and then the statement will be repeated.

1.

2.

3.

4.

5.

Comprehension Multiple-Choice

Complete the following conversations by choosing the correct answer from the options listed.

Track 32

1. Un, *deux, trois, quatre, cinq, six...*
   What comes next?

   A. *huit*

   B. *dix*

   C. *sept*

   D. *neuf*

2. "Poussin, poussin, you say the sky tombe...
   Comment tu le sais?"

   A. *Je ne sais pas.*

   B. *La poule* told me so.

   C. *Le cochon* fell on my *tête!*

   D. I saw it *avec mes yeux!*

3. Whose idea was it to go into *la tanière?*

   A. *L'éléphant*

   B. *Le renard*

   C. *L'oie*

   D. *La mante*

4. Which of the following are insects?

   A. *L'oiseau et le serpent.*

   B. *La feuille et le ciel.*

   C. *Le patio et l'arbre.*

   D. *La mante et le papillon.*

5. How would you say "Here I am" in French?

   A. *Je suis ici.*

   B. *À bientôt.*

   C. *Merci beaucoup.*

   D. *Au revoir.*

Now go on to complete the reading/writing portion of this test.

🔊 **Turn the audio off.**

Matching

Choose the statements that match and draw a line to connect the two.

1. butterfly

2. cave

3. tree

4. mouse

5. garden

A. *souris*

B. *papillon*

C. *jardin*

D. *tanière*

E. *arbre*

True or False

Write T or F for each statement.

_____ 1. *Une feuille trés grande* fell on chickie's *tête.*

_____ 2. *Le poussin* thought the sky *tombe.*

_____ 3. *Les animaux* asked chickie, "Comment tu le sais?"

_____ 4. *Le poussin* responded, "Je suis ici."

_____ 5. *La poule* told *les animaux,* "Allons nous-en!"

Answer Key

1.

2.

3.

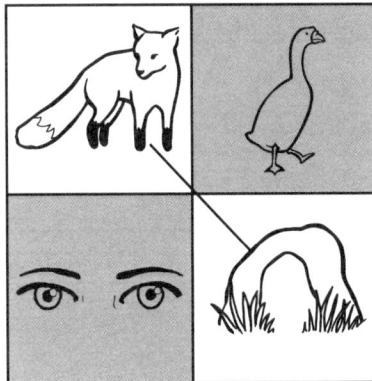

4.

5.

Comprehension Multiple-Choice

1. C. sept
2. D. I saw it avec mes yeux
3. B. Le renard
4. D. La mante et le papillon
5. A. Je suis ici

Matching

1. B
2. D
3. E
4. A
5. C

True or False

1. T
2. T
3. T
4. F
5. F

Recipe

Ratatouille

1/4 cup olive oil

1/2 tsp garlic powder

salt to taste

2 onions, sliced thin

1-2 small zucchini, sliced

1 small eggplant, very coarsely diced

1 red bell pepper, seeded and coarsely chopped

1 yellow bell pepper, seeded and coarsely chopped

2 ripe tomatoes, peeled and diced

Pour 3/4 cup water into a large, nonstick skillet. Add the olive oil and garlic powder and bring to a boil. Sprinkle in salt to taste. Add all of the vegetables to the pan. Bring to a boil and cover. Cook for about 30 minutes over medium heat, stirring occasionally, until the vegetables are thoroughly cooked and the water has evaporated.

Serve hot, as a vegetable dish or as accompaniment to grilled meats.